to you,

- hannah.

BookLeaf
Publishing

India | USA | UK

Presentation by *BookLeaf Publishing*

Web: www.bookleafpub.com

E-mail: info@bookleafpub.com

ISBN: 9789358735574

First edition 2023

to præy on a star

my mother once told me
that you could wish on stars
which fell from the sky
a streak of white against black
just a moment passing by

i remember wondering to myself
why we wished on a dying flash of light
why we preyed on falling stars
why we prayed to God day and night

what Father makes suffering a trial?
what Father makes His love a mercy?
what Father, who is so based upon love,
makes me, His child, feel like he could not love
me?

but who am i to speak outright against Him?
who am i to doubt the boundless love He
harbors?
does God (my præyer from heaven)
ordain my damnation in His holy orders?

and so i sit complacently every sunday
singing and worshipping and bringing praise

clasping my hands and bowing my head
to pray as prey for the rest of my days

with idle hands, a thought slithers in
hooked into me as if i were a fish
it asks me, quietly, what makes the difference
between a prayer and a wish?

once, i saw a star
small and bright and dying
i cupped it in my hands
a wish in its purest form vying

that night was quiet
save for the blood rushing in my ears
my entire body shook
isn't this what i had wanted for years?

but the word 'want' has never lingered
it never felt right for it to stay
it always got stuck in my throat
so i tried to keep it at bay

have i never wished for a thing in my life?
(have i ever felt like i deserved it?)
was i doomed from the start by fear?
will i always be paralyzed by it?

and so i swallowed it whole

like a greedy little child
i choked it down with my want
holy, tender, and mild

maybe i had thought it'd save me
rid me of this sin that burdens me so
a cleansing salvation the consumes with light
with a too full heart in tow

and i wonder when i die
if God will pry me open and see
my heart, the star, my want
and choose to not forgive me.

to believe in a dying concept

in my life, there is a through line
seen as a thread of gold
stitched by the hand of God
made to bind me in a perfect mold

His Son take my hands in His own
punctured by the persecution from those before
me
He smiles gently down upon myself
but the light reaches neither his eyes or me

an empty yearning choke me at the apex of my
throat
with hands gripping salvation with desperation
they grip so tight i fear i will mar the skin of our
Lord and Savior
(perhaps, then, I am not so different from my
forefathers as I had imagined)

there is this gaping feeling inside me
that i try to fill with every God-filled task i can
find and see
think that maybe if i did, i could trick myself
into believing

(and even if it didn't fool Him, maybe He would
at the very least forgive me)

(God, i wish it was easy)
(God, i wish i knew what to do.)
(God, I wish I knew who I was
outside of this person I have crafted
with fabric cut from the cloth
and sewn together shoddily
with the threaded through line in my life.)

this thread, however, is gilded to look gold
but it is only performative, and yet the truth still
remains
knowing it was only a thread did not revoke it so
i was still bound in a web of His Mercy all the
same

to my mirror

time blurs past me like brush strokes on a
canvas,
colors bleeding together
as i lose grip of reality.
who am i?
it reverberates against walls and the void
i gaze into the looking glass,
but the mirror has been smudged,
only a marred visage to look back.
i feel like the worse version of narcissus,
looking to my reflection to tell me what it is i
see.
am i only a parent's daughter?
am i only a friend to those i hold dear?
am i only a disciple of a God whose word i defy
just by living?
is all i am just in conjunction to another?
am i truly even my own person?

(who am i?)
i look down at my hands,
stained with a myriad of colors with no start or
end.
is this who i am?
an artist lost in her craft?

an artist who pursues not her passion in fear of
losing it —
in fear of disappointment —
in fear of expectation —
will i always be a slave to fear?

(who am i?)
i am...
someone trying to exist
in this hard to exist world;
someone whose bed can feel like a tomb
that, too many days, i wish i could lie in;
someone trying to find joy in a place where
happiness feels frail;
loved.

(who am i?)
i simply just am,
and that is enough.

to the yearning in my chest

and i ache for you
in a way that confuses me
because you're still here.
you're still tangible.
you're still alive.
you're still in every crevice of my mind,
in every thing i touch,
in every sight i see.
you're still here.

and yet, you're not.
you're not here at all, are you?
because the words
that came so easily around you
instead lodge into my throat
because the solid reliance
of you next to me
instead becomes an empty mirage
of smoke and mirrors
because the question of
'when will i see you again'
becomes
'when will you leave again'
and my heart who would swell
at the thought of you

swells to the point
i feel like it will burst until i die
and yet it's just shy of
because i could never exist
in a world without you.

and i miss you.
i miss you so much
that it makes my chest tight
and makes me want to hold onto you
so you can never leave again.
but that's not love
to keep something
because you're scared of losing it.
but this isn't love either, is it?
because i've already lost you
and i'm the willful fool to your whims
because anything is better
than losing you
even if it's a lie.

to unbecome at my own shortcomings

i will always miss you
in ways i am still learning
you are the sudden loss of air
the death in which my heart goes yearning

but i'll scrub myself raw
until my skin is pink and bleeding
until i'm someone who you've never touched
with wounds i am, even now, still treating

but i suspect it's my fault that i'm like this
that i'll never let someone know me truly
but maybe a self-fulfilling prophecy is all i need
to convince myself i'm right to protect me

(love me, i scream, fight for me to stay)
(piercing through my head)
but not a sound comes out
until you're just a silhouette in my bed

i sleep with ghosts that are not my own
grim figures that haunt over my dreams
but in them, i see myself just like them
sunken, and fraying at all my seams

it's easier this way — better, even
this way, the only person getting hurt is me
but for as flimsy dreams are, they do not lie
and all i find in them are hurting memories

to my unfailing despair

i will never escape being sad
no more than i can escape being happy
but the chance of sadness looms heavy
like a desolate rain cloud
crowding densely over the sun
it looms and it taints and it haunts
until my life is no longer highs and lows
but just lows and the anticipation thereof

there's always a reason to be sad, i say
(though i'm not very sure who i'm trying to
convince)
there's dwelling on the past, mulling the present,
and fear for the future
what is there not to be sad about?

and so i let it all unravel
until it plateaus into a long, desolate line
where there is no high, or low
just anticipation
and the lackluster feeling of being right to
anticipate despair

the yarn tangles when it passes
muddling my memory as all that takes over

is just my own sickly sadness
it winds in a tight ball that loops through ribs
constricting my chest until i take air in half
measures
the only thing strong than my despair
is my resolve to staying with it

it is so tiring to be sad.

to drown at sea

the key to learning how to swim
comes first with learning how to float
it's an easy enough skill to learn
to lay on your back on open water
lazily watching life go on around you
and so you learn to float, and it's as easy as
breathing

it's less easy to decide to stop floating
where you become suddenly afraid of everything
and you're fearful that you will seize up
before you even get to swim
and so you stay afloat, but so does that fear

and the fear, you soon find, becomes heavy
not all at once, though at times it feels like it,
but gradually until you feel
that the decision to stop floating will kill you
and so you stay afloat, because you are afraid
of what happens if you don't

you lay there, half submerged in water
watching the clouds drone by slowly
you wonder what it's like to be like that
instead of the heavy burden in your chest

and you stay afloat, despite it

but this a weight lodged between my ribs
feels like it's going to sink me until i drown
down
down
down
i thrash for a lifeline —
i panic for just one good breath —
anything —
just anything —
anything to get me free —

if a tree falls in a forest
(if i drown out at sea)
and no one is around,
(and no one ever knows)
does it still make a sound?
(am i actually drowning?)

control slips from me as i slip from reality
and it is in this where i find myself
the most at ease i have ever felt.

to have known you

much like my bed
my heart is too big for just me
but i'm scared what i'll let in
will hurt me in ways i can't see

so i lay in a corner
curled small, despite the vast expanse
because i've never learned to take up space
and so i never gave anyone a chance

even you, to whom i've spent my love
are kept an arm's length away
i pretend you are in my heart
a lie that grows looming day by day

it is not hard to listen
to ask how you are and listen with intent
when you tell me about your life
and i ask you what you meant

it is harder to talk, to me,
of things that actually matter
i pretend to be transparent in virtue
instead of a façade of broken glass shatters

i will love you, in time
and you will know me, someday
but all days, i'd rather you didn't
so i will leave, and you will stay

i'm sorry to have known you
for who you were, are, and will be
when you were fooled
into thinking you knew me

to have lost you

im not sure what i can say to you
we are all changing, all of the time
and yet this sickening pit of dread
that sits right above my chest
stays unmoving, unchanging, unbidden

maybe it was our proximity that drew us close
and the fact that you were seeking stability
while i was seeking something fun
the pit of dread coiled around my ribs, then
knowing it would never last,
but hoping that it would

i wish there was something more
something tangible i could tell you
but it's always been close to nothing
with empty words and placating pleasantries
as you showed me all of you
and i showed you none of me

the pit lingers
as best as i try to pretend it's not there
but it's lighter, i think
ever since i've lost you
and while it is a cruel sentiment
it was the same truth
that i was always too afraid to face

to love both ways

i wonder if it will ever stop
with the way i love you
for it consumes me whole
i hope i never hear of it
and
i hope you are well
because i love you
always, always
but i am aching
i know time means to heal
still, it never stops hurting
and
in a way
i still love you
despite everything
and
despite myself

to scar over love

my friend had told me once
of beauty marks being indicators
of a past life's love
it didn't hurt to believe it
so i smiled and i teased her
about the mole on her left ring finger
she rolled her eyes at the time
swatting me before changing the subject

over time, i noticed a similar mark
forming on my own left ring finger
it was innocuous and simple
only could be seen when my fingers separated
but it was hard to ignore
and i found myself looking at it
more times than i could ever admit
(even to myself)

it became a nervous habit of mine
to rub at it absentmindedly
as if i was trying to remove a stain
and eventually it grew into me picking at it
until i was trying to excise it from my skin

it didn't bleed then, but even at that moment

i knew it would scar
a tiny mark on the sloping plane of my skin
that would remind me
of my first instinct to love

there was something to have been said
about the symbolic nature of it all
of love forming physically on vessels for it
and the blatant removal and subsequent scarring
but at the end of the day
i still wished i could erase myself whole

to be or not to be

i often grapple with the idea of being enough
of being too much or too little
of overcompensating or undercompensating
i often feel like i am paying recompense
for everything wrong with me
and when i try to make up for being too small
i instead become too much

i wonder who you'd be without me
or, better yet, if i ceased to exist
in truth, i've always thought
that the world in and of itself
would be better off
so i figured as beings
as inconsequential as we are
would benefit should i lack existence

i've never been one
to say i want to die
it felt tangible and dangerous
to speak it aloud
and it didn't feel real enough
to attribute it to how i felt
even if i did want to be gone
even if i did want to not... be

and, truth be told, being take work
as does all things worth doing
but it is so hard to exist in a world
where you brain only fathoms
it being better when you aren't there

but there is a beauty and love in being
that flushes my cheeks pink with laughter
and a bliss i could find nowhere else
but with the people beside me
so, to be or not to be?
that is the answer

to hold onto love

the problem that lies in my love
is that i want so deeply
that it becomes rooted in fear
because i could not fathom something
(someone)
leaving
and so i hold with a grip that scars

(don't leave.)
(please don't leave.)
(please don't leave me.)

with it comes that incessant fear of change
change of the unknown
change that will come with you
finally realizing i'm not worth your time
finally realizing there are better things to do
than to entertain a girl long past her time

so i smile and i laugh and i try to lift you
pushing down any little thing
that might cause reason for you to sway
maybe if you are distracted by my love
you will fail to notice the desperate grasp
of a girl who is too afraid of being left behind
and too proud to admit it

to let go

i'm not sure what it is
i'm letting go of
but i suspect it is everything
i have ever kept within myself
in this tightly wound pit
at the center of my chest betwixt my ribs
fraying and unraveling but never failing
(i wish my resolve to be happy
was half as strong
as my resolve to be sad)

with a scarring grip
i finally pry my fingers free of it
and i let it unravel between my fingers
belatedly, i realize
that the only thing that has scarred
is me, with deep crescent grooves on my palms
bored through with my desperate resolve
with the feeling that if i ever let go
i would drown

my fingers ache the way they do
not unlike ones coming out of a too-long cramp
free, my hands sing, and free, my tears fly
i had forgotten how to feel so light

that for a moment i am afraid i'll float away
but my ship rights itself
and for even just a moment
even if after all this i will be scrambling
for my tightly wound thing of despair
i relish in my moment of reprieve

to float

i've always viewed floating as precaution
a measure done to save yourself from more
dangerous perils
an exercise to my fear of the unknowing change
as the reason for floating became my reason for
sinking

it's different now — now that i've realized a few
things
things like how letting go is exponentially less
scary
things like how holding onto things can harm
you
things like leaning on those around you
to prevent feeling like you're slipping

it's a bit scary, admittedly, to float
to feel so light you think you'll fly to the ends of
the earth
but it's scarier to be bogged down
to be pinned until there is no way to go up

and it is okay to not to be okay, because
everyone finds land

and grounding yourself before your head is in
the clouds
is an exercise to a fear of the unknowing change
(there are, after all, some things that are harder
to shake)

to almost love

i have never known love in the way most people
do
(the way it is reciprocated in kind,
and not some one sided, unrequited pining
affair)
but i find that the thrill of love still remains
and the camaraderie amongst friends
who whisper and laugh and tease alongside you
are the center of the moments you actually
cherish

i have had my fair share of rejection
and of cold confessions given long after its fact
i've had my long list of crushes
its popularity growing in my girlhood
but growing older makes you realize
that there is love in simpler things than people

love in any capacity
is not a grand lightning strike
of coup de foudre
but starts like a pebble
each special moment amassing into a
sentimental collection
one day i hope i have enough
to replace the once heavy burden in my chest
with a heart with a weight of endless pebbles

to live

i feel, as if, i will always amount to
something short of enough
with my breath catching
before my lungs are full,
and with my heart swelling
until it is pinned behind a cage,
like i am filled just to the marked line,
only meant to survive and not to live

i don't want to end up
a shell of what i should be
instead of who i could be,
i don't want to end up
simply having wandered aimlessly,
wishing i had done more — done less
been more — been less

but i am scared that love is finite
that i will never have/do/give/be enough
and i will be doomed to shelter my heart
in fear of the greater unknown
never known to love
and never known to be loved

but maybe all it takes is time

time to understand how to live
time to mull over the gravity of my self
time to forgive myself for just being
i've never been one to dive in feet first
but this fear is drowning me right on land
so for once
— for once —
maybe it's best i jump into the deep end

and it's a shoddy attempt
the way i am trying to practice
how to love and how to be loved
(i hope you've noticed)
(i hope you can see
how surprised i am to be happy)
(i never thought i'd live this long)
(i never thought i'd have been happy)

at the end of days
i hope i can say
i have been loved
even if it was just by me.

to be alive

the hammock sways
gently back and forth
like rocking a baby to sleep
a leg out barely touching the ground
adds to the momentum
as i lay face-up to the sky

the night around me is restless
voices howling over the crackling fire
wildlife chittering in its nature
but only the night's nipping chill
catches me in its snare

i hear them swapping stories
trading tales in the firelight
laughs that come straight from the belly
wrap me in a blanket of content warmth

i can see the stars
bright enough for once
to finally see a constellation
my chest rises and falls
i hear them get ready to call it a night
crickets and owls make sounds alike
oh, what it feels to be alive

to the moon

oh, how i've gazed upon your face
fond and reverent and altogether holy
you come in different phases
and yet you never cease to surprise me

you are grace pooled in the wide open sky
a sliver of hope smiling with infinite eyes
stories are woven through you endlessly
while you are a story regaled from inception to
demise

there are stories where you love the sun
whether it is by blood or by soul
in this truth, the story will never waver
but, as stories oftentimes have, there is a toll

it is not the love that feels like it'll kill you
it is the infinite distance betwixt the light and
mirror
that will do you in longer after you have set
but even at rest, you bleed into the day to see her

and there are stories where you love the sea
the same distance that kills the both of you all
the same

but some days you are so close together
that you think that alone will be your bane

but you never falter or fail to rise
and though you go through phases, as we all do
there is no point to deny that
you are beautiful tonight, aren't you?

to me

from years ago, where you were writing near
daily
in a journal you kept to the side of your desk
i'm not sure how to say that we'll have forgotten
about it
only for a short while, until something happens
and we go running to it with fervent handwriting
(we tend to be bad at breaking habits, after all)

reading back on it, it feels almost trivial
seeing me react to things like
giving class notes to a boy we liked
or being upset we disappointed our teacher
where it felt like big reactions to small situations
but i know they were big at the time
and oftentimes they still feel that way
so i smile and think fondly, and turn the page

i forget how sad we were
it's not as obvious amongst all the trivial
moments
but i remember how small we felt (and still feel)
i remember the feeling of hopelessness
(i don't know how to tell you it never leaves)

reading some of the pages makes me wistful
it feels like you're curled up next to me as i read
cheek pressed against my arm but with your face
turned
(you hated people reading your notebook,
but your eyes still seek to know their reaction)

i wish you were right next to me
i wish i could have hugged you the way you
wanted
but still didn't let anyone do
i wish i could tell you it gets better
i wish i could tell you it got worse before it got
better
i wish i could tell you every bad thing that will
happen
i wish i could tell you every good thing that will
happen
(you will meet so many people who love you)
(you will love so many people)
(you will love yourself)

but i can't, because you're not there anymore
but i hope that somewhere you hear it and you
know it
that you will be happy (and maybe i'll believe it
too)

to you,

i wish you well
(i have always wished you well)
in ways, i wish i did not love you
i wish that you did not sink so deep
into my bones, heart, and soul
where i am suddenly affronted
that the horrifying ordeal of loving me
comes at the cost of knowing me

so i swallow my fear
(and i swallow my pride)
and slowly i bare my heart
even though you have already resided there
but for you, i will have hollowed it out
just to make room for you
just to be sure that i will always have room for
you
i find you're already home there
and i am content and blissed
even though i know
i will never be whole again if you ever leave

but that is love
(as much as every issue inside me yells against)

to remove the safety net of keeping one at arm's
length
to submit to being known
it is the act of giving yourself
and showing who you are in actuality
and pray they do not turn from you

so, to you, i have hollowed my heart out
to you, i have left myself on display for your
judgement
to you, i bare the vulnerable cavity of my chest
and pray you do not turn your head in disgust
to you, i give you the deepest recesses of myself
so that you may know me
(so that you may choose to love me in good
faith)
to you, whom i trust
to you, whom i love.

(even if i am never whole again,
i pray i am at least always with you.)